all the broken things

Geoff Inverarity

Anvil Press | Vancouver

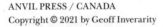

ANVIL PRESS / CANADA

Library and Archives Canada Cataloguing in Publication

Title: All the broken things / Geoff Inverarity.
Names: Inverarity, Geoff, 1951- author.
Description: Poems.
Identifiers: Canadiana 20210227028 | ISBN 9781772141757 (softcover)
Classification: LCC PS8617.N84 A85 2021 | DDC C811/.6—dc23

Cover image: Ryan Heshka
Cover design by rayola.com
Interior by Derek von Essen

Represented in Canada by Publishers Group Canada
Distributed by Raincoast Books

The publisher gratefully acknowledges the financial assistance of the Canada
Council for the Arts, the Canada Book Fund, and the Province of British Columbia
through the B.C. Arts Council and the Book Publishing Tax Credit.

Anvil Press Publishers Inc.
P.O. Box 3008, Main Post Office
Vancouver, B.C. V6B 3X5 CANADA
www.anvilpress.com

Printed and bound in Canada

To my parents, Leslie and Priscilla, and to my family.

Thank You

My thanks for years of support from many people, without whom, etc, but particularly the following: Tom Snyders for producing all those readings, from the one at that Laundromat on Main Street to the heady days of the Tongue of the Slip, George McWhirter, Peggy Thompson, AnneMarie MacKinnon, Brian and Karen at Anvil Press, Hilary Peach for pointing me to Anvil in the first place, Miranda Pearson, Joanne Randle, and Jana Davis. And for the enduring friendships of Alan and Sue, David and Margaret, Linda, Mike and Anna, Edi, Steve and Helen, Kenny, Nick and Kareen, and Geoff. And for the generosity of my Spanish families: Joe and Cari, Zak and Jolee, and, of course, Rafa, Nuria, Andrea, y mi hija española Luna. To Barton Hewett and Howard Dancygyr for hours of intense conversation, to Roger Semmens, Gary Geddes, bill bissett, Stephen Roxborough, George and Karen Harris, Lee Trentadue and Jim Schmidt of Galiano Books, and, of course, to the whole Galiano Island community. And, finally, to my children, Max, Spencer, and Imogen.

Table of Contents

TO: BRIAN KAUFMAN
ANVIL PRESS

The Gulf Islands Gardening Column

Galiano Island
Next Year

Dear Brian:

In these days of environmental crisis, I am often asked to write
about country living, and to share some gardening tips. It's
hard to know where to begin, but perhaps I should start with
some extracts from my diary.

I should also tell you that nature revolts me. No. Nature mutat-
ing to Garden revolts me.

Troubling
material
this.

*Landscape as text. (Re)writing the ecosystem: words exclude, engulf,
inscribe: "weed," "wilderness," "flower," "garden," "park."*

June 1

This year, I intend to devote myself to my relationship with the land, the planet, the universe; survival in this material context. I will internalize nature, store it, become a conduit, pour it out again. I begin this diary in that hope. Out of the stuff of this forest, I will rebuild my psyche; my brain will be filled with the trees and the creatures thereof; their needs, desires, and fears. Their terror. The process begins here. This island, my Walden.

Already I am beginning to write like Margaret Atwood! All these strings of variations, additions, explanations!

Linguistic imperialists pushing back the frontiers of language; drawing lines to cross. (Dis)cover a new(found)land. Writing: limits. Pushing back frontiers, we dig out an abyss with/out limit: space as difference. Postulation: (a)void: "frontier," "survival," "garrison," "develop."

June 13

The weather still does not break. The heat builds, nature stirs, erupts, comes crawling out of the woodwork, literally.

A million winged black half-inch long Carpenter Ants swarm out of nowhere, from hollow trees you never saw before. Landing, they crawl about, frantic, monomaniacal. They never fly again. They bite their own wings off and leave them to be eaten by other, tinier ants. The Carpenter Ants are looking for mates.

They deconstruct; they are excavators, mining wood, carving out territory; they construct, making space. They like cavities. They mate; the males die. The females convert their useless wing muscle into eggs. There is a profound metaphor here, although I cannot quite articulate it. For two days they will cover the walls, inside and out, though these concepts are meaningless at this stage. The night will fill with the ghastly rhythm of their wood gorging, the scrabble of their disgusting little feet, the clatter of their hi-tech armoured bodies.

Listen.

They are remaking your house.

Break   silence.

Listen: the white man is here to hear the tree fall in the forest at last;
to declare the end of silence, the beginning of "silence." The white
vacuum is broken: here is pen, here is paper. Lines hiss across the page
finally. Writing: "civilization": narrative: "seasons," "harvest,"
"priorities," "treaty."

June 18
I wake spitting out ant wings. It has begun. Ant Day is behind
us, but I fear an ant is within me. I hear its giant jaws chewing,
the pounding of its enormous feet. My sense of balance is
disturbed by its blundering movements. It must have dropped
from the ceiling, its momentum carrying it deep within my ear.

June 23
It has been confirmed by the Committee.

There is a Carpenter Ant inside my skull, gnawing at my
brain. There are things I no longer remember, although it's
hard to say what, since I no longer remember them. So this is
what it means to lose your mind. My skull feels half-empty.
Half-full, rather. I must remain optimistic, yet it hardly matters,
since I cannot tell which half is which. "I" am being rebuilt.

Internalizing a void; absence. Nature is devouring me,
creating an abyss in my mind. There is room for forests,
granite, savannas. It is a dwelling place for unborn monsters.

June 28
As the old popular song says: "There's a membrane lining the
lid of my skull where my brain used to be,/Yet I'm thinking
more clearly each day." My head is the planet turned inside out.
The sky is a carapace, the earth the hole in a donut. Existence
is absence. I am eager to see how this will end.

I had not expected things to turn out quite so literally.

July 1 Canada Day
Glorious weather; the tea things laid out; company expected.
Daisy in that *special* hat. Jamboree at the North End. Fun for
the whole family and Sunny the Clown. How we all laughed!

I cause a stir by eating the Community Hall. So soon after all those expensive renovations!

So this is what it means to be a Canadian! I have to say it: I am proud to be a part of this great land!

Writing: narrative: the Story of O/Canada. His/story has it that Nature likes it rough in the bush. Men read what Susanna Moodie wrote first. They like the idea of all those thrusting spades and binding fences. Writing: "discover," "map," "survey," "property lines," "foundation," "walls," "outside," "inside," "house," "garden," "writing," "lines."

So, how is life in the city?

And what are people wearing?

Grief

Grief's a bastard
Turns up no notice on the doorstep whenever
moves in doesn't shower doesn't shave
won't do dishes
dirty laundry
eats badly spends hours in the bathroom
keeps you awake half the night
shows no consideration
puts a filter on all the views
no matter how sunny it gets
the place still looks like shit.

Grief's a bastard
talks long distance drinks too much overmedicates
can't finish a book
keeps flipping channels mutes the sound
turns down the colour
till it's all washed out
faded away.

Grief will travel anywhere in the world to be with you
nothing too extravagant for Grief
can take the whole sky
paint it bloodred demolish cities
call down storms
turn forests to sawdust
punch holes in mountain ranges
bedroom doors.

Speaks for you
whether you like it or not
roars furious flails around
when you ask him how things are the fucker tells you
trails along behind on walks
dead-eyed pathetic shuffles

till you wait up and turn
taking a deep breath
knowing what's coming.

Gets old acts distant suddenly doesn't call for weeks
then comes over with too much whisky and
a bag of crappy skunkweed
just to keep you on your toes.
Jumps you in an alley after a movie
and while he's beating you says
we must keep working on this relationship.

Afterlife

— *What do I remember my father saying? I remember him saying*
"I can't be bothered with all that nonsense."

The grass is luminous with an unfamiliar sheen
as my father, a straightforward man from birth,
steps up to the first tee
on a golf course he's known all his life,
shoulders square
looking for his line
as the wind comes up from the sea and moves the grass.

Alone with nobody ahead
no one behind he stands
with time to consider the sphere of the ball
its nature, the cavities daubed on its surface
like drops of water seen from the inside,
the way the sinuous fairway unfurls
swoops away to the right
towards some hidden flag

and time to count the trees and all their leaves
their strangeness and the divots like jewelry.

A concern in the air brushes his cheek.

His shot goes high and long
the arc crosses the rim of the horizon

climbs
until he can barely make out the circle of the ball
against the crescent of an early moon
hanging in the nonsense of a concave sky.

The Codgers' Lament

We have seen the typeface shrink,
the printed page recede, shivered,

and waited for blood work.

Every day brings more horrific news,
every day brings the exhausting gruntwork
of putting on these GODDAM socks and FUCKING shoes.

Each morning feels like the weight of concrete
poured over our bodies squeezing our spines
like wheezy old accordions.

Everything else feels as if
it's been beaten with a stick.
Where did they come from, all these welts and bruises?

Some invisible bastard did it
in the middle of the night
the same time as our looks got stolen.

Meanwhile our minds stumble and stutter.
Names won't come,
words start to flutter away won't

stay on the page, won't
stay the course; they
keep getting away from us.

Words have begun floating just out of reach
in a damp midway past shrouded stalls
full of rigged games and terrible food.

In the gloom, there's one badly-lit booth still open
where they play a strange game
we don't know the name of or the rules

though we're hoping to learn,
but the hands of the dealer are moving too fast.
We have found to our shame there are things we can't follow.

A small crowd is gathered there, feeble of limb,
agéd of face, skin like raw beef, nameless people
we may have seen before though it's been years, and we can't be
sure.

A message finally appears
scrawled across a scrap of paper,
strange letters none of us can read,
words in a language that nobody speaks.
Now, too late, here, at the end of everything,
we are given a message we can't understand.

At this point, there's nothing left to do
except turn to face the music.

Face the ancient music,
face the ancient music and dance,
do the inappropriate dance,
do the wild dance,
dance defiance,
and **dance,**
dance,
DANCE.

At the Three Artists Show
(Galiano Island, August Long Weekend)

The photograph: outside the gallery
away from the crowd, chairs on browned grass,
the end of the day, drinks, three men, a woman. Old friends.
One, Morriss, his mind fading,
a cigarette between his fingers,
looks at the camera,
a little baffled, already not quite *there*,
already partially submerged in the growing dusk,
and gone soon after.

A memory: Santa Monica Pier, July, sixteen years ago, evening.
The Bubble Man making bubbles for tips
long grey hair, a beard
tie-died T, cut-offs, sandals.
You know the type.
He works whatever hours;
he pays his rent.
I tell him my little daughter's first word:
"Bubble." He nods, smiles.
"That's a good word."
She chases his disappearing art, laughing,
part of the show.

The Ferris wheel is lighting up.
His buddy comes by:
"How's it goin'?"
"Uh, you know. Just easing into the evening,"
says the Bubble Man.
"Easing into the evening."

In the telling of tales
even of grief and great loss,
in accounts of back-breaking pain,
there is a certain joy in telling it true,
a task well performed,
in landing the right word in the right place
at the end of the day,
in a sentence well turned.

Old friends
that time of year
the arbutus splits its skin
chairs on the lawn
the golden hour fading
the end of the day.
Just easing into the evening.

The Afterlife of Lobsters

The saddened fish farmer is trying hard to teach us
about his salmon — how to eat them;
surprised at customer resistance, he concedes
"Most people don't know how to relate
to a one- to three-pound salmon." Indeed.

It's hard to relate to a one- to three-pound salmon —
in fact it's almost impossible.
You have to think of floating in black wet air
lungs full of fluid flashing and flashing
as you turn in the salmon pens
muscular as a tongue,
hearing muffled alien voices from above.
Moving in darkness, knowing feeding time
and diving into light. And after months in darkness
a sudden release gasping out of your element
from fish farm to freezer thrashing towards death.

Yes, it's hard to relate to a one- to three-pound salmon.
In fact it's almost impossible
though at times I have felt like a lobster
in the supermarket near the fish and deli section
within snapping distance of the tartar sauce depressed
repressed oppressed helpless hopeless pin-eyed
flopping body heaving powerless claws
caught crawling
making plans for breakouts
shooting the shit with other lobsters
just to pass the time.

But there's always something happening here,
and all in all we've had some good times here.
And joy — yes, joy; I would say we have known joy.
Our lives are full of event, and besides,
when it is time to leave this little tank,
we will find that place I have been told of
where lobsters gleam and swim in seas of liquid gold,
where lobsters shed their shells forever,
their tiny eyes grow wide and claws spring free unbound.
There crustaceans have the grace of dolphins
plunging through a shoreless sea.
There the morning bite will never end
there we shall swim forever
as free and strong as salmon in that sea of molten gold.

Last Night

I dreamed it was midnight
in the shopping mall
one damp summer night
and I was getting an early start
on Christmas shopping
even though the card and wrap selection
was minimal.

And as I dreamed on
I dreamed
I was Laurie

Anderson
and that my voice rose
and fell
at inappropriate moments.
And as I dreamed further
I found myself

pausing

for no
particular
reason.

I dreamed on
and found myself
pausing
at the wide open doors of the shopping mall
looking out over a lovely Japanese landscape
carefully, perfectly

prepared.

Rehearsal for the Millennium

It was New Year's Eve and the time
was midnight
when your ex-husband
french-kissed and fumbled
his new girlfriend
while her old boyfriend
who was there with his new girlfriend
looked uncomfortable.

It was a time
when only parties mattered;
when rooms were filled with ex-wives and ex-husbands
and husbands and wives about to part
and lovers. There were hordes of lovers.
And lesbians. The place was swarming with lesbians
and lovely men other men dreamed about
and couples who only dreamed of one thing
and that was to be unfaithful
as often as possible
as soon as possible.

The time was neither here nor there
and women, tired of lies and laundry,
drifted back from bedrooms
smelling of love, weed, and each other's perfume.

Hard Living

it's hard living on an island, especially when your molecular
structure's as unstable as mine is

some days it's so bad i can't i can't i can't speak
my teeth are chattering so much and i can barely write
it's like the old joke about the woman on her honeymoon sending a
letter to a friend p.s. please excuse the shaky writing

there are advantages

my lover (who's been very supportive throughout it all) says it's great
for sex, and if i ever go critical, an island's the best place for it
i wouldn't want too many people to get hurt
in addition, because the frequency's so high, i never have to worry
about household pests, or even raccoons and some days i can reheat
small portions of frozen food in my mouth
i miss having a cat or a dog, though

i go to town a lot these days; i find the noise and the traffic and the
people restful
with strangers it's easier to be intimate

in the city i pack a laptop, you never know, it doesn't do to take
chances, not with such a thin ozone layer and the way the ice is
melting

most of these visits i spend hanging out drinking draft at
Mandelbrot's, it's a hotel on the south end of Granville
the gravity's vicious down there but when they switch on the strobe
lights sometimes everything seems to come together for a minute or
two and i reach a genuine sort of calm
don't laugh

but i'm also there because i know Jake will be there, and when you're
looking for some equilibrium, you want to know where Jake is

equilibrium

it's a virtual reality app that's all virus

a rogue rampant psychosis that's compatible with all known platforms
some dumb hacker tripped over it trying to access his mother's biopsy
   results
it's dangerous stuff; i'd be the first to admit it

makes heroin look like, well, like heroin
that's the beauty of it and the horror — everything looks exactly like
itself and nothing is ever the same twice or even once

the universe is remaking itself every instant

everything

morphs

there is no possibility for metaphor
the dimension of symbols has ceased to exist; everything is exactly
   what it is
you can see that symbols are only symbolic after all
that words only mean one thing and then only once, then they get
   changed, remade
look for a different, an alternative, a substitute and each one is just itself
and you learn that you can only use a word once then it's changed
forever, bigger than it used to be
after all, language is part of the universe

it's always expanding and the space between words just keeps getting
   bigger
i can never repeat myself

i can never repeat myself
so now when i say i i i am writing the i back in wrIting
do you see?
do you *see*?

equilibrium

Jake gives me a look at what's in his briefcase and for a second
there i feel existence winding up for something really spectacular

but he snaps the lid (white rhino hide trimmed with monitor lizard
— that's **style** man!) **shut** and i'm back on south Granville at the end
of my seventh draft and the seventh draft, believe me, is nothing like
the first

when the waitress turns around you can see from the heat on her
face that she got a look at what's back inside the briefcase

she's keeping her eyes on us because it's part of equilibrium's
properties that users can flash out of sight and turn up three days
later or more a month maybe a year a century
how could we know

hooked already
the cops usually get them home in a hurry, if they don't croak right
away, that is; they have their orders

people say the government knows what's going on

they say equilibrium was developed by NASA's alternative fuels
division after the Challenger blew up
but i don't buy that one
once you've run equilibrium, you know you're looking at something
that's been with us forever, something old as time, older maybe

i start another draft, a new one, and my flesh is crawling, my eyes
are beginning to melt out of my skull, i'm wiping lumps of soft hot
jelly off my cheeks, the waitress is still watching us because the light
show when you phase out is fantastic, they say

it's a form of turbulence, a phase transition

you go from stability to chaos but there's no point of departure
it's another dimension, more or less where you fall into an infinite
system of bifurcations no matter how closely you look you see the

possibilities are endless every second every fraction of a second
every fraction of a fraction of a fraction of a fraction of a fraction
and nothing is ever the same twice or even once

equilibrium

right now every particle in my body's oscillating so fast i can barely
hand Jake the five K and the promissory note for my firstborn
malechild that buys me three minutes

we both know that next time i'll want five and he'll get ten

we both smile
he's thinking organ transplants; i'm grinning like an idiot because i
know i couldn't get pregnant even if i tried, not with my ovaries in
this state

on my way home i tell myself that this time it'll be different,
naturally, this time i'll wait for a coupla days, but the tiny drive is
already beginning to squirm and nuzzle against my skin and the
reality pull even now is terrific
you don't mess with molecular fever

equilibrium

i'm a special case
not an addict exactly
i'm luckier than Jake, luckier than the poor bastards who get caught
in a time loop, because they never find out what's happening to
them and happening to them and happening to them

entropy gets them in the end
they just wear away

listen

i've seen things that… i've been places… no, let me tell you…

it's hard living on an island, especially when your molecular
structure's as unstable as mine is
some days it's so bad i can't i can't i can't speak and i can barely
   write
it's like the old joke about the woman on her honeymoon sending a
letter to a friend p.s. please excuse the shaky writing

oh you heard it before then

listen

it's hard living on an island, especially when your molecular
structure's as unstable as mine is

listen

it's hard living on an island
it's hard living on
it's hard living
it's hard
it's
it
i
.

Second Growth
(for Jana)

It's sixty years since the last logger left

hauled the last boot
out of ground that sucked on him
like a fifty-dollar whore (he'd laugh
as the mud parted, just
so
for an instant
a vacuum opened under his feet
the power of place not letting him go
as he hovered, beatified, uncomprehending
poised on a bubble of nothingness
blessed before the open grave snapping vicious
at his hard young virgin's legs).

All that wrenching in the time of death forgotten.
Time was when the moment rested
its steel-tipped toecap
on the precision of a cut
the heft of an axe
the rip of a saw;
time was when it was all worth more
on the ground.

Somewhere in those fifty years
the raw skid roads turned to alder.
Man, you should of seen that alder come back!
Like rockets.
Overnight the firs and cedars were spikes
hammered up between the stars,
while on the ground, the green crept back
and the sweet dark water still
rises and falls in the old camp well.
Rises and falls
rises and falls.

The Sessional Lecturer's Lament

Labouring without dignity
walk in classroom
temporary
sort of.

Hands soft
empty
full of dubious values.

Indicate smears on palms:
ink from broken printer.

Black ink
on pink hands.

This is an image.

NB BREAK ICE

Make Morning Joke:
academics, getting hands dirty, blah, blah, blah.
Hint at
hands exhausted
calloused by pencils.
Worn out
after turning all those pages.
Weak eyesight (e.g. Milton)
blah blah blah.

Audience remains dubious.
Knows inkstains when it sees them.
Knows that's not
real dirt.

Today we will examine
the inkstains of Others.
Again.

Project voice over low incessant hormonal roar:
Truth is beauty; beauty, truth.

Questions?

Will that be on the exam?

That is all you need to know.

So why can't you get a real job?

The Possibility of Fire
(for Roger)

It's fun working with you —
I admire the way you deal
with the spite of the mundane.
There's the way you handle tools,

the long easy silences.
I heal as we read the wood,
laughing at the art of seeing possibility,
all the possibilities of fire.

On days like these,
with the sun drawing steam from the cedars,
everything makes a little sense at least.
There's a delight in knowing
we can see lines then step
across them,
knowing how much closer
we can come to one another
down at the old marble-hard rings
of the bucked maple,
driving a wedge between us.

Canadian Doctors Pioneer Permanent Implantable Artificial Heart

There are never enough hearts to go around
to heal the damage life exacts,

so the heart market is booming.

In quiet laboratories the makers whisper about life

perform small adjustments on slick valves

and the smooth, miraculous, inhuman tubing
that mazes through a heart more easily broken,
but on the other hand repairable.

Doors open, close,
inevitable valves marking the rhythm
of human progress,
while research continues in other areas
where these manufacturers of hearts excel.

Here the company magicians build simulators
for those who are learning to fly,
where imagined gusts of air sweep
over easy-sprouting dream-wings soaring through an ageless,
shapeless eagle-heaven

Further down the hall,
keystrokes on the virtual-anesthesiology simulator
cause an imaginary patient to slip into imaginary sleep
filled with blazing jewelled artificial visions
of imaginary dreamtime.

At the press conference,
the triumphant parade of the heart begins.

At first it will carry the old heart piggyback, explains Dr. Tofy Mussivand.

The little machine itself is absent from the photograph
which catches Dr. Tofy open-mouthed
one hand extended as if about to grasp something.

He is looking at his hand.
His hand is empty.

Perhaps he has just dropped the first permanent implantable artificial
heart (on which an
                estimated 20 million dollars has been spent on research.)
Oops, he is saying. *O shit.*

Perhaps he is just having one of those clumsy days we all have
when our lives go a little out of control,
or a lot.
When cups of coffee flood the kitchen floor like aneurisms,
or when we drop words we never expected to say on our lovers' heads.
Oops. O shit.

Dr. Tofy's fingers grasp the air.
His mouth is open,
his hand is empty.

Nothing has been dropped; the heart remains unseen.
Perhaps Dr. Tofy, like the rest of us,
is just extending himself to hold, however briefly,
everything
silent
everything
invisible.

My Mother's Haunting

My mother kept a clean house, even after she died, suddenly, from a massive stroke. Luckily for my father, left alone in the house to take care of himself, spare bedding was neatly folded, ironed, and stacked in the linen cupboard beside the water heater, each sheet, pillowcase, or blanket individually wrapped in a heavy plastic bag, sealed with sticky tape, and bearing — my mother's haunting touch of genius — a self-adhesive label pointing out the date each thing had last been washed.

Thus, when I arrived, bewildered, jet-lagged, and grief-struck, I was able to find exactly the right combination of thoughtfully itemized bedding, while my father could sit, red-eyed and weepy, beside her empty chair in the living room. I took the dust sheets off the furniture in the bedroom I had used far less often than she would have liked and made up my bed with a matched set of fresh sheets, crisp pillowcases, and clean blankets.

She was still there then, only a few days dead, hovering in the convergence of plastic, sticky tape, and labels, directing the show, organizing us. During her life, the habit became something of a compulsion. She threw away nothing that could ever be used again for anything, no matter how inconvenient, ugly, or unsuitable. Empty margarine tubs would reappear under plant pots to catch the water; the lids of yoghurt containers or coffee tins would make triumphant comebacks, gaily transformed into handy drink coasters by the simple application of tartan mac tack; any wool left over from the sweaters and scarves under perpetual construction was immediately knitted into small squares, the squares sewn into blankets, and the blankets wrapped in plastic bags, dated, labeled, and sent to the Children In Africa.

And she was still there, seven years later, when I took another of those dreadful transatlantic flights. This time, my father was in Intensive Care, sporting a colostomy bag, heavily sedated, half gutted, and greatly reduced in himself.

I found myself alone, I thought, in my father's empty house, except my mother was there again, a phantom in the linen cupboard, asserted by her neat and rounded girl's boarding school script. She was still the ghost in the machine of household tasks, those small renewals and re-orderings that sustain us, leave us free for the vast and dirty business of living.

The bedding was ready, last washed well over seven years before, but still fresh and well wrapped. As each seal was broken, my mother disintegrated a little further. My niece, who had picked me up at the airport, remarked on each label, in baffled awe of so dedicated an engagement with entropy. All those hours spent on keeping a clean house; all those thousands of hours spent folding and ironing, as if the forces of disorder were ever massed outdoors, pacing and snarling in the raspberry canes, waiting for an unfinished task, for the defences to come down.

She kept those spectres of anarchy away as best she could, their reality scarred into her being by the stalking horror of having lived in the midst of global warfare. When your experience of life includes such terrors, then you had better know where your life jacket is, you had better be prepared, you had better have the blankets ready, be on guard — for the cataclysm, the earthquake, the explosion, the flood or famine, the sound of the air raid sirens, the thunder of invisible bombers, cancer, a stroke, or perhaps even the discovery that there is another woman in your husband's life.

She was real, that Other Woman, and I have learned that she was there for over twenty years, her solid shadow falling across the needlework no matter how big a bulb my mother put in the standard lamp above my father's empty chair. Now I am drawn back in time to watch my mother, alone in the house night after night, and I am forced to watch her turning up the radio to cover the sound of nails tapping at the window; I am beside her as she spends her days alone, wiping, dusting, scrubbing and polishing. I see her as she finds a plastic bag, one of the ones she never threw away, and wraps up the coffee pot or glassware, or the napkin ring, writes out the label, seals the bag, and packs it away. Then day after day, she freezes and dates the leftovers from all those uneaten dinners because my father had been late home from work (Beef Stew 03/02/87;

Shepherd's Pie 25/10/88; Strawberry and Apple Pie 07/03/89), as well as the peas, raspberries, and broad beans gathered from the garden in the last summer of her life; then she can reline all the drawers and the cupboards (paper, thumbtacks, and a dated label); take the leftover fabric from the curtains she just gathered and sew it into a matching bedspread, make new lampshades out of pressed flowers and clear plastic, even reupholster the dining room chairs, until every thing is marked, accounted for, and controlled. I hover, invisible by her side, because we have reached the point where all there is left to do is to find one bag big enough to cover the whole house and all the rest of us in it and write out a label that says, like all the other labels: "This is my house, these are my children, and this is my husband. I will never leave."

I am like her now, writing this, keeping disorder at bay in my own way; telling a story; putting a little more design into the chaos of my own experience. I am still breaking the seals today, on a package of my schoolwork; on a christening present from a long-dead godfather, a silver napkin ring engraved with my initials, cherished, wrapped in a small plastic bag and lovingly labeled with the date of its last polish.

Each seal broken is another breach with the past; but it is also another chance to remember her, touch what she touched, thank her for all her work. And as each seal is broken, I imagine another small release for her, because her work is almost finished; soon, none of this will matter, and it's long past the time for her to rest.

Max (Aged Two) on Pebble Beach, Galiano Island

His tiny ship goes out each day
(I hear my mother sing to me)

> *Bobby Shaftoe's gone to sea*

from unknown continents
he hands us treasure

> *Silver buckles on his knee.*

mysterious stones
secret feathers.
At night we sing to him
promises

> *When he comes back, he'll marry me*

a mockingbird, a looking glass.

> *Bonny Bobby Shaftoe.*

Read this one day, darling
if you cannot understand why our hearts ache.
You might hear the echoes
of promises our hearts made

> *Bobby Shaftoe's bright and fair*

promises

> *Combing down his yellow hair.*

our hearts' promises.

> *He'll be my love for evermair,*
> *Bonny Bobby Shaftoe.*

Listen.

Grandad, Like a Huge Ear

Grandad sits in his all-too-easy chair,
enjoying the flight in his fashion.
Captive, curled in on himself
like a huge ear,
he listens, he listens, to his captain, his heart.

This is your captain speaking.
In case of an emergency,
there are no exits,

and our cabin staff is helpless
in the face of the inevitable,
as I, your captain, also am.

Our estimated time of arrival
is any day now,
but shortly a meal will be served.

There will be an arbitrary interval,
then we will serve a continental breakfast,
and we will keep serving continental breakfasts
until the flight is over.
Any day now.

There is no life jacket under your seat.

In the unlikely event of a sudden drop
in cabin pressure,
we will all die.
Although I might be mistaken about that one.

You may now put your watches forward
or back.
As you please.

Grandad, like a huge ear
curls in
curls in
seeking to become
perfect
as a shell.

In Memoriam: Dr. A.D. Fuller (d. 1986)

That night (perhaps the night before)
I dreamt a map of Africa
pencilled on a scrap of paper.
The news was that the Gambia
where you lived and worked for all those years
had been invaded.

Lines drawn showed the direction of troop movements
coming in from two flanks.
Rushing in to fill a vacuum.

In Sussex, you, poor little aunt,
were lately lost in your mind, mapless.
Out wandering alone, lonely,
in a place where diagnosis was impossible,
through an empty hospital's
dull catacombs of corridors,
through rows of empty beds.
You'd just lost the thread.

That night (perhaps the night before)
heading for nothing, the fireball went up
over Florida.
The news was that the Challenger
had exploded.
"Uh oh."
"Obviously a major malfunction."

Perhaps that night,
perhaps the night before, heading for nothing,
the fireball in your mind burst,
erasing the hospital, burning clean the beds,
immolating the fear of being lost.

Obviously a major malfunction.

You killed time lately
doing nothing, mostly —
long walks in gumboots and a mac
in West Sussex,
a place where maps aren't needed, mostly.
Africa a memory.
The future nothing more
than long walks getting older.
The past a panicked ocean
receding frantically.
So you trudged on, redrawing the map,
inscribing great fat zeros on the countryside.

Childless, children were your life.
In those scorching jungle days,
the lines stretched through the trees.
Mothers sitting patiently, days, sometimes;
who'd carried baby's stools for miles
wrapped in cloth for the doctor,
magic woman, who would divine
from what baby'd passed, baby's future.
They waited for the word of life and death from you.
I would have thought that nothing
could have wiped that out.
But then nothing did.

I could remember, try to give you back the past.
Even then, though, nothing filled your head.
At dinner one night, talking about the Great War, you said
"Millions died." Shouting now:
"And all for bloody nothing.
Nothing." Banging your hand, tears in your eyes.

You were there.
You liked to joke, and I knew your name at least,
though as a child I could not say Aunt Angela,
and called you Annie Ashes.
Others, grown ups, called you

Doctor Fuller, Doctor, or Angela,
but never, sadly, love or darling.
I, grown up, don't know what to call you.
Naming seems redundant.
What are you?
What should I call you, now my aunt is ashes?

Oh, Aunt.
Though nothing filled your head,
and the vacuum's pressure crushed you,
though you divined your own future
and saw nothing there,
to me
you were really
something.

Happiness Slides

It was an ill wind maybe that whipped in
from the Indian Ocean that evening,
when clouds covered the sun,

and the coral that sprouts in the day through the sand
to scour the blind flesh of your soft tourist's feet
raw as revealed secrets
was covered by the waves.

She and the child, hand in hand
leaning together with courage into the wind,
so far south and close together
with death by water.
There was spite intense as magic down there in that ocean
enough to make you fly off your feet,
to inhale you like dust.
And the air was tinged with salt

and a haze of blown sand covered the world,
vague as too much gin.

And did they feel the sea opening then?
What was it they cast on its waters?
What did they leave on the sand those days
with the headaches and the beach toys

and the sunscreen and after
the child was asleep when did the evening go wrong?

I wanted to drop the camera, drag them
like an undertow back from the void,
but the shutter fell again,

and it wasn't enough that I only had them forever.

Still Life, with Scissors

After my mother died
I went out looking like that.

I put my feet up on the furniture
and didn't put my clothes away.

I threw away the string and wrapping paper
and didn't put those in water.

Got a pet.
Didn't feed it.

Soon, without waiting to hear what my father had to say,
I drifted into the lonely kitchen

opened a drawer with awestruck miniature fingers
took out the good scissors
three steps across the floor

outside to the strange, unfamiliar garden
where the lawn stretched halfway to the horizon
and the moon blazed.

Still looking like that,
I took a deep breath
and began to run.

Looming

Everybody's talking
about The Looming Pointless Catastrophe
how pointless it is
how much it looms.
What a catastrophe it's going to be.

We're stockpiling for the short term
the long term we don't know.
No matter how much you prepare
there's always something new looming
like the Unexploded Grief Bomb
we found buried deep
out in back of the house.

It's been there for decades
we figured a previous owner
but I'm not so sure.
Besides, it's ours now.

It's on some sort of timer
we have no idea.
Thing is, it's going to blow
sooner
or later
(hard to say which would be worse).

Someone else's Grief Bomb
went off down the street last night
there were sirens, lights, and weeping.
So there's that.
We know about that.
We'll take a casserole or something
as one does.

I have to admit
I resent all this Looming.
Try not to, but there it is:
life's a bomb on a timer.

Traffic Reports in Strange Cities

You're driving into a city you've never been to
with the radio on
listening to a traffic report
about roads and places you've never seen.

Got the radio on

Everything is exotic, mysterious, potential —
bigger sales, better service.
It's all better, sleeker, more exciting,
more modern than that provincial dump of a town
where you live.

Radio on

…because it's another beautiful morning here in the foothills!
That makes fourteen in a row! But who's counting?
And now, here's traffic with Jen Holster.
How're things on the road this morning Jen?

Thanks, Andy.
Things on the road? Well, they are not looking good, my
friend. Not looking good.
Be warned, commuters! Heavy, heavy volumes.
Everything moving very slowly
from the Benchmark all across to the Navigants.
And maybe you'd want to avoid the
Bypass Memorial Bypass
Bypass today
after that big oyster meat spill.
At least keep your eyes open for the seagulls.

And the cars keep coming.

Got the radio on

Traffic's seriously backed up
from The Celebrant's Mall
past the Brief Sojourn Funeral Home,
beyond the Young Paupers Cemetery
past the gates of the Old Fever Hospital.

Radio on

Detours back in place around the Zoo
even though most of the monkeys that broke out
have been apprehended.

Crews are sifting through the rubble for clues,
though we still don't know
how the monkeys got the guns and ammunition, or the drugs.

And the cars just keep coming.

I guess everybody's heading down to the Marmite Centre for the
big game.

Go Roadrunners!

Got the AM Radio on

Andy, I dunno, man,
the cars keep coming and coming
and nobody knows where they're coming from.

OK, you should be thinking ahead seriously to this evening, people.
There's no way you're making it home
with this volume of traffic.
I dunno. I really don't.
I guess you better
you better
please just leave work early;
remember the curfew's still in effect,
and the Army have orders to shoot on sight.

That Was the Night
(Doug "Doc" Randle 1928 - 2013)

He was just a skinny kid from Calgary.
laid up in bed for the best part of a year and a half
in terrible pain, isolation
all the joints swollen
eyes too sore to read
hard to swallow, nausea, fever,
no school for the duration — not that he missed it.
It was wartime and he was marooned
surrounded by the dark songs
of the vicious prairie winter
moaning around the house.

Until late one night he's alone
with the radio on beside his bed
scanning the aether

'til something comes in
from somewhere down in the States,
maybe some freak of the atmosphere
bouncing across the invisible border
off the Northern Lights perhaps
making him catch his breath his heart race
hearing something he'd never heard before
wilder and kinder than the winter's music
something soaring, something lifting him up.

Without warning he is hurtling east
leaving the mountains behind him
he skims over the dead wheat fields
hard as a gravestone a blur beneath him
the night streaming by
until suddenly there are skyscrapers up ahead

crowded sidewalks the streets filled
with yellow cabs, neon glimmer, and steam from the grates

just like in all the photos
except in colour now.
He knows where he is
feels the deep grace note rumble
of the subway beneath the magic city.

Life! It was life like he'd never lived it
out there in the dull Canadian West.
He swoops low, hurtling along
the chasms between buildings
riding the beat honing in on a trumpet
holding a single breath-defying note
just for him so's he can follow the sound
he knows the way now
c'mon in kid!
He's beckoned down some stairs to a basement club
where these black guys are blasting
after hours icecool hepfire jamming
up on the tiny stage elbow to elbow
chops are flying
the whole place packed, steamy,
all those wild hep cats in zoot suits
transformed, possessed, delirious.
The shady wise guys with their dames
rejoicing with whisky and reefer
steaks and spaghetti
he feels the bass hold him steady,
before the fat guy on the piano showers him
with notes like confetti hooks him
and the whole joint in and reels them up
so high they say goodbye to gravity

floating in a cool void where the saxophone
shoots starbursts cracks the night sky
wide open and everything blazes.

Even the band can't believe what's happening
the drummer throws back his head

howls because he's hearing impossible music
nobody has ever played before
creating the universe again and again.

Too soon, the radio signal fades into static
the pain and the isolation grind back

and the snow piles up outside
except now the skinny kid's infected
with something rare, something new
knows there's something he has to do
never mind the music teacher
to hell with Fur Elise
the pretty Mozart tinkles
the Beethoven bombast
the dumb high school drama.

He's elected.
Here is freedom, here is flight
here is life shouting
here is where the journey starts.
He has to get back there to fill the void
drown out the static
lift himself up, lift us all up
make his own way be the one, the many,
the starlight-maker, the joybringer.

That was the night he heard music from the future.
That was the night Doug Randle heard jazz.

Max at Montague Harbour

There was
there was not
a summer evening
once only in the infinite history of the universe
when the planet aligned itself exactly for us
against the sun.

Everything brimmed.

And my son's presence was absolute, unyielding, eternal,
the pressure of his weight against my shoulder
holding as it did a radiance of trust.

After difficult years
he seemed to return his flesh to me
so that we might have mingled again, beings impossibly
melded.

There was communion then
despite knowing
that as my body, this mass of particles and forces,
took on his child's weight for life,
our electrons were dancing apart

and we were two magnets flinging away from each other
into the void.

And that is how things are:
we need to oppose each other,
to know this fundamental repulsion we call touching.

Then, under our feet, ancient pebbles, clamshells;
the driftwood hard at our backs;
between the mountains cut out of darkness

the trees stacked on the cliffs behind us
the bay being cut by a single powerboat.

And these things happened:
the horizon tipped
and the last of the sunlight poured over earth's rim
sheening the bay
with the eloquence of waves
rushing silent through space;
then there was the sudden unasked glory of light flashing
speeding across the water towards us
as the sun caught plumes streaming from a waterskier's heels
turned them to jets of fire
at last, after all those millions of years.

A Prayer for Our Sons at Nine
(for bill bissett)

BOOM!
and the boys are back
hungry and transgressive
with their graffiti their downloads and their dreams.

mr max and mr spencer! most xcellent! says bill
hey bill they say because
they know cool and bill is cool.

They pour in the room
keeping their boots on
filling space
until the creaking windows bulge
walls crack and burst
with the power of all their cranked up joy,
their fierce, terrifying love.

They straddle borders
between centuries
now and soon
between my body and yours
brothers and friends

and their song will be the tearing up of passports;
they will dance with lightning in their hands
on magic rainbows, fearless, ecstatic

their story will be the story of the end of all boundaries.

Let them teach us
everything is permitted
remind us how to break the rules;
let them bless us with their riot,
let them make us look like fools.

For I Will Consider the Child Cyrus

Songs quoted are from the 2007 album *Hanna Montana 2: Meet Miley Cyrus.*

For I will consider the child Cyrus.
For I must consider my daughter Imogen on her seventh birthday.
For my daughter Imogen grows in the shadow of the colossus that is the child Cyrus.

For the child Cyrus is two in one, one in two.
For she is the rockstar Hannah Montana, here to rock the world although the world knows Hannah Montana does not exist.
For Hannah Montana is the child Cyrus, and Cyrus is Miley, daughter of Billy Ray.

For my daughter Imogen whose world at six years had not yet been rocked is now rocked.
For the child Cyrus carries the party within her.[1]
For now my daughter is rocked thanks to the child Cyrus, who tells her she can turn a park into a club[2]

For the child Cyrus believes in love.[3]
But sometimes it's not so easy to draw the line.[4]

For bad things as well as good happen in the blink of an eye.[5]
For Miley, like everybody, is not perfect. [6]
For the child Cyrus implores us to peel away the surface dig down deep beyond the clothes the makeup and the world that is show.[7]
For the child Cyrus tells my daughter that everybody makes mistakes.[8]

---

1. "We've Got the Party (With Us)."
2. Ibid.
3. "Bigger than Us."
4. "G.N.O. (Girls' Night Out)."
5. "One in a Million."
6. "Nobody's Perfect."
7. "Old Blue Jeans."
8. "Nobody's Perfect."

For the child Cyrus tells her that she must work it again and yet
again until it's right.[9]
For the child Cyrus acts out stories of loyalty and compassion and
loves her dad.
For she is an instrument for the children to learn benevolence upon.
For the child Cyrus sings that life is what you make it and she has
made the choice to make it right.[10]

For I will consider the diction of the child Cyrus.
For she sings that she has fallen into the "yarms" of the one[11]
and she would have us take her "As I yam"[12]
For Cyrus is not perfect, but knows that she is not perfect.[13]
For the outside is not the inside and we are not our mistakes.
For there is nothing wrong with just being yourself.[14]

For my daughter Imogen,
named from *Cymbeline,*
knows, like Shakespeare, that looking good and being good
are not the same thing.
For she knows that the image and the person are not the same thing.
For she knows she is unusual and no one else can stand in her place.[15]
For my daughter Imogen one day may be the Tai Chi practising
snowboard champion who fixes the flat on your tire on the Arizona
blacktop in the blazing sun when things have never been darker.[16]

For my daughter knows she is Imogen Moon Randle aged seven,
blessed with two brothers,
and she will be constant and filled with courage all her days.

---

9. Ibid.
10. "Life's What You Make It."
11. "One in a Million."
12. "As I Am."
13. "Nobody's Perfect."
14. "Make Some Noise."
15. Ibid.
16. "Rock Star."

That Was Her, My Grandmother
(Jessie Brodie Inverarity)

In those days, like the other women in Edinburgh, she only bought
what she could carry in her bag with one hand
a struggle if it was a big shopping, but worth it, she thought,
if the grandchildren would maybe just come for their tea.

No cars for them, those women,
just a walk to the shops was all they'd manage,
across the pavements, made from slabs
of cold hard stone from the savage north,
foot-worn, smoothed by years of steady passage.

Leaning into the relentless wind, that was her, sure enough;
the needles of dark rain jabbing.
The gloomy days in winter were always harsh and short,
while the long dark nights lingered like an old cough.

That was her: like them, those women, modest,
heads covered, undressed outdoors without a hat,
a big wool coat, thick stockings,
and sturdy brown shoes that lasted.

Her days were spent in solitude
a widow from the Great War.
Her two sisters away in Canada emigrated years back,
for herself a son, two grandsons and a daughter-in-law.
Just one close friend,
a cousin, but they had fallen out —
there had been some sort of pointless feud.

You know the sort of thing
confusion, just a missed appointment
in a cafe for a cup of tea and cake
but my grandmother
was left in Crawford's for a good half hour just sat waiting.
Well! That's that!

These days a few seconds on cell phones would have sorted it
    out of course,
but in their day, with no telephones at home even,
a frigid distance opened between them,
a chasm, an ill feeling that grew steadily worse.

She held stubborn to the grudge as only relatives
can, and my grandmother promised
*Well that's that. I'll never speak to her again
as long as I live.*

So that was her until that moment somewhere inside her brain
when the blood stream flooded its banks.
She never put her shoes on any more
never walked out to the shops.
The years from now on passed without season,
her head was sheltered from the wind, the rain.

No need for a coat or hat
as nurses came and went with bedpans, catheters and
terrible food and the visitors passed by on their way
to something else.
Because that was that.

As the family gathered round her bed to wrestle
with the crisis of the first terrible hours after her stroke,
from the bed opposite
calling out across the space between them
the voice of my grandmother's best friend,
now bed-ridden, crippled, hands like claws, arthritic,

her dear cousin Margaret who
had left her sat waiting for
a good half hour in Crawford's,
all of a sudden asking *Jessie? Is that you?*

Then that was her trying to reply
engaging for the first time
in a doomed battle with words.
Suddenly it was too difficult to get her tongue
around even the edge of speech
to find a sound remotely like a name
in this new mouth someone else's mouth
turned into a strange unknown place
all undergrowth and traps
where she couldn't speak any language
an endless dark cave
filled with a tongue that seemed
turned into a great wet piece of cloth
crammed into her mouth
flopping desperate, soft; a dying fish.

And from then on, that was the two old women,
placed in beds side by side, a few feet apart,
sat all day and all night, year after year,
inseparable, waiting till death picked out one of them.

But my grandmother, Jessie, had no more words to give,
she was doomed to keep her bitter promise.
I'll never speak to her again she said
as long as I live.

The Way Things Are

My son and I are bonding.
A big improvement on when I picked him up
from his mother's last week.
He was radiating embarrassment beside me
like an atomic device of doomsday proportions,
all my good intentions were anti-matter to him,
immediately annihilated by his presence.
The fallout is global, the contamination lingers for centuries,
so I have a lot of explaining to do to my neighbours.

If only I could remember his name! At least it would be a start.
John? Ken? Duncan?
Duncan sounds familiar.

By way of breaking the ice,
I ask him what he plans to be,
what his dreams are, his aspirations,
what peaks he will conquer, what stars he will touch.
Will he walk on other planets as I have dreamed of doing?
Will he be remembered in a thousand years
for his contribution to our unending story?

But what can he do?
He comes from a generation
convinced that all the doors are closed,
the resources exhausted, the exits jammed,
that the place is filling fast with poisonous gasses and toxic wastes.
And of course they're right.

Plus, as any fool knows,
all the poems have already been written;
there are no paintings left to fill the empty canvasses;
every piece of wood, metal, and stone
has been carved, hammered, or chipped away to nothing.
All the books have been written;
all the possible words

placed in every possible order;
there's nothing left to say,
and no words left to say it with.

All the films have been filmed,
the dances danced,
the songs sung;
the last notes of music are fading into the vacant air.
There is no art left to make.
Art is at a full stop,
period.

As for diseases, they're gone too.
There isn't a sick person left on the planet in need of care;
there are no more hungry people to feed;

and nobody's homeless any more.

Doctors we don't need now,
and nobody ever needed lawyers anyway.
The prisons are all empty,

and torture has been eradicated
along with all forms of political repression.

Multinational corporations are now
head and shoulders above reproach,
while the whole field of mental health care,
once an ash-strewn wasteland
filled with a vast crowd of twitching, scratching, drooling, scabrous,
terrified people picking at themselves,
everything from barking-mad, willy-waving maniacs
to toothless old women rocking themselves to death
in their own exclusive hells;
this whole field is now an empty expanse of lush green meadows,
spangled here and there with the occasional exquisite
daisy.

I don't know where to start with the boy.
Even the criteria for maturing seem to have changed.
Maturing used to be a process of learning stamina
emotional and intellectual
so that you could deal with complex systems
of behaviour and art.
Focus, that's the key.

So what do I tell him instead,
now that stamina's no longer required,
that relationships are for better only
and when the worse comes, you move on;
when a thirty-second cut is a demanding piece of art;
when you terminate your on-line conversations
every time they take a turn you don't care for;
when the channel-changer's just so damn handy;
when if you don't catch their attention
in the first five seconds you're passed over
for something flashier, something faster.

All that time spent learning to control your mood swings
when you were eight years old.
What's the point?
Whenever you feel uncomfortable,
even a little,
log off, medicate,
hang up, move on, medicate,
cut the connection.
There's no need to feel bad if you don't want to.

Tonight, I add, there's going to be a lunar eclipse,
but not for me.
The alignment which produces it will be over
before the moon ever rises over this house.
The curvature of the planet
and the usual time zone nonsense take care of that.
In the year 2050, the same thing will happen again
except it won't be an identical event,

there aren't two of those in the universe,
as if you had to remind me.

It goes on and on, the universe,
cranking out events, but it's not so smart.
The universe may think it's pretty great,
but no matter how big it gets,
it'll still be dumb, dumb, dumb.
The stars are rushing out and out and away
without any idea of what's about to happen
in the long run.

They haven't clued in
that there is no perfect alignment,
and, better still from my point of view,
no cosmic chiropractor to make the adjustments this place needs
to make its deadlines, follow its schedule,
turn up for all those appointments on time
with no excuses about stopped clocks.
This is time in action,
raw time,
time in its purest form, dependable,
deeply entropic.

I'm going to be out there waiting with my watch for the next eclipse
saying *So what the hell happened to you?*
You're always late!
This just isn't working for me.

There's a point, I suppose,
when you begin to realize
that there's going to be a day
that's going to start with you
and end without you.

This eclipse will happen again
in the same way, almost,
in the year 2050,

and it doesn't take a rocket scientist
to figure that I won't actually be here
to not see it again.

It's not coming around again, this eclipse, for me.

You know what's so depressing?
When you figure out
that *everything's* a once-in-a-lifetime experience.

I should tell the Boy to remember all this.
Turning sixty, he'll hear about the lunar eclipse
and remember our conversation.
Or not.

All the certitudes fall away from me as I write.
I could say that I plan to make him remember.

Like a curse or a self-fulfilling prophecy,
certain moments haunt us because we've tagged them.
We'll set the alarm, make a note
in the calendar of the rest of our lives.
He'll remember what I tell him;

for a moment the past and the present will coexist,
as if we took a fold in time's fabric
and pushed a needle through,
pulled it tight.

And I'll be there, right beside him.
It's the best you can do if you want to live forever.

I remember the days when there was no end of fun
when the future stretched on
well out of sight, like a highway in the desert.
Somewhere over the horizon was our destination,
but the road itself was all ours,
and the traveling of it went on.

I used to even think I'd be there
when the parallel lines met,
now I'm not so sure.
Now I'm looking down the road,
wondering if I'll even cross the horizon,
let alone reach the single strip mall and the gas stations
and, just beyond the light from the street lamp,
under a crackling blue neon sign,
the small dark bar
where there's always time
for one more drink.

I'm telling the Boy all this,
but he isn't grasping a word.
Not a syllable.
Soon he can go out and play
with his protoplasmic little friends,
but first there's work we have to get finished here,
and I'm not done explaining things yet.

My Mother

I lie awake in this huge empty bed and console myself by remembering my mother, a beautiful woman. Hers were not your run-of-the-mill Marilyn Monroe/Tilda Swinton sort of good looks, but transcendental, glorious, the kind solar systems are destroyed over, the type of beauty which gives rise to cults, mass suicides.

When my mother walked down the street, elderly matrons fainted, staid businessmen clapped their hands over their mouths as their eyes bugged out, and they screamed, biting hard into their palms until the blood flowed and even then it wasn't enough as they fell to their knees, arms outstretched, imploring, howling lust, pledging eternal servitude.

Toddlers who'd scream when daddy held them ripped themselves out of the arms of their devastated young mothers. Eyes gleaming, they'd waddle, chortling across the road, traffic chaos, screams, mayhem, faces of pure joy.

It wasn't easy being me as a child; there was a *lot* of competition — from other children, from waitresses, bank clerks, clergymen, nuns, and movie stars; supermodels and customs officers, politicians and disc jockeys, physiotherapists and psychotherapists — Freudians, Jungians, Adlerians, Lacanians, and more.

Her admirers included world leaders — Jack Kennedy was particularly insistent, as I recall — figure skaters, artists, singers, writers, and plumbers. She was a big hit with the homeless, as well as with astronauts, deep sea divers, welders, airline pilots, flight attendants, movie producers, makeup artists, caterers, and grips. Academics from every discipline, cowgirls, the insane and the mildly neurotic, the terminally ill and the newborn, bored housewives and their workaholic husbands — they all adored her. She was coveted by stamp-collectors, murderers, and bird watchers, bicycle couriers and motorcycle cops, masochists and sadists, heavy-metal guitar players, heroin addicts, firefighters, and heavy smokers, people who drank too much coffee, the anorexic and the bulimic, as well as judges, gardeners, poets, construction workers and art therapists.

Nobel prizewinners drooled over her, jazz drummers sighed at her, princesses groaned after her, critics dreamed and cried because of her, fishermen wanted her, strippers deeply longed for her, loggers hurt and thirsted for her, professional escorts stalked her, personal bodyguards craved her, aerobics instructors never got over her, widows, spinsters, bachelors, and the happily-married hoped, yearned, aspired, and itched for her; lesbians pined and gay men languished; chiropractors went mad because of her, hot tub salesmen killed for her, massage therapists worshiped her, and drag queens wooed her.

But for her, there was only . . . me.

The Last Time I Saw Elvis, He Was Buying Disposable Razors

The last time I saw Elvis, he was buying disposable razors —
the kind for sensitive skin like John McEnroe used to use. The
time before that, he was handling baggage at the Greyhound
Bus Terminal in Seattle. He'd lost a lot of weight, he'd grown a
big moustache, and his hair was in a brushcut. He had more
tattoos than I remembered, and he spoke with a Brooklyn
accent. But I knew it was him.

(Elvis is everywhere.
Elvis is a circle whose circumference is infinite
and whose centre is everywhere.)

When Elvis fixed my muffler, I was a hundred miles east of
Reno, a hundred miles east of a bad memory, just this side of
Heartbreak, only a change of clothes and a brokedown Chevy
Nova away from Oblivion. Fifty bucks in my pocket I won in a
craps game, a bad taste in my mouth, and a shoulderful of
broken promises. I was in no mood for trouble. He did a good
job on my muffler. Really. And he didn't overcharge me or
carry out any unnecessary work. That says a lot about the man.

(Elvis was the expectancy and rose
of the fair state.
The observed of all observers.)

In the years since his death, Elvis has bought me fifteen beers,
total — on three separate occasions. He cut my hair in Wawa,
Ontario, and once sat next to me at a lunch counter in the
Combat Zone in Boston. He had a cheesesteak and a Diet
Pepsi. Twice he invited me for Thanksgiving — though both
times I was busy. Plus he arranged a loan for me with his bank
manager at very competitive rates, helped me get off amphet-
amines, and surprised me by turning up on the beach in
Mexico, eating *ceviche*.

(Hare Krishna
Hare Krishna
Elvis Krishna
Hare Elvis)

In the bar of the Gresham Hotel in Dublin, I bought Elvis a
double Bushmills — figured I owed him for all those beers —
while he explained his breakthrough work on superconductors
to me and its implications for the fields of Artificial Intelligence
and cancer research. It was exciting stuff, I can tell you.

(Introibo
ad altare Elvis.
Elvis giveth the peace
that passeth all understanding)

Right now, Elvis is in the kitchen, fixing eggs. Not just a great
singer, the guy flips them over so easy, the yokes are always
perfect. Also, he makes the best damn chili this side of Austin.
And his johnny cakes just melt in the mouth. After we have the
eggs, we thought we'd catch a movie. He's getting the movie; I'll
buy the popcorn and the soft drinks. He could do with the
break after all that work in Afghanistan.

A lot of people think I'm nuts. But I have tasted those johnny
cakes, and they are not of this world.

Nazis in the Supermarket
(in memory of Paul de Man)

*Within hours of the death of Rudolph Hess, Spandau's only prisoner,
who committed suicide by strangling himself with a piece of electrician's
cord, the Allies announced that the prison building would be torn down
to ensure that Spandau would not become a rallying place for neo-Nazis
in the future. A supermarket would be put up instead of a prison.*

Nazis in the supermarket
checking out the bargains
in the cheese section.
Lingering over the liver, eager
to plunge old arms in it to the elbows
and stir the whole bloody mess up once again.

Nazis in the supermarket
hate to stand in line.
Putsch past pregnant women at the checkout desk
demanding prompt service.
Saying Nazis before all.

Nazis take eighteen items through the express lane,
staring down the checkout clerk.
Nazis gather in groups by the soup aisle
hissing in each others' wizened ears.

Nazis changing the Best Before stickers
on the kosher cold cuts and the cottage cheese.
Nazis regrouping under cover
of the magazine rack,
swapping stick-on tattoos with their chums.
The word goes out, whispered round the paper products:
"The Reich shall rise again."

Nazis in the supermarket never forget.
Elephantine memories run amok,
charging at the past.

There was a summerhouse once in Spandau,
and an old, old man whose cells had split
and died and died,
had died fifty times;
at the age of ninety, he had died fifty times
and then there was a piece of electrician's cord,
left there by accident, on purpose,
or by benign neglect.

Half of fifty Hesses have sat here
where cord and body came together,
where Albert Speer was a gardener.
Hess is not a gardener. After Speer left
the garden thrived on benign neglect.

If Hess ever forgets
his past lapses,
does the present moment of remembering
now being a blank render obsolete
the personality responsible for the past?

His past his story history:
read the texts of Rudolph Hess.

Suffering from Brain Poison after the war
a Hess simulates loss of memory
until it claims a miracle:
after days of only water,
laced with Brain Poison,
a glass of wine (which it only pretended to drink)
revives its mind.

"I was permitted," says the Hess at Nuremberg,
"to work for many years of my life

under the greatest son whom my country has brought forth
in its thousand-year history.
Even if I could, I would not want to erase
this period of time from my existence.
I am happy to know that I have done
my duty to my people,
my duty as a German,
as a National Socialist,
as a loyal follower of my Fuhrer.
I do not regret anything.
If I were to begin all over again,
I would act just as I have acted,
even if I knew that in the end
I would meet a fiery death at the stake."

Later, one claims: "For three years
they caused my intestines to close;
they started to add corrosive acids to my food.
The skin came loose and hung in little bits
from my palate.
They put itching powder into my laundry
and glass in my dessert."

Now Hess is the essence
of peace and quiet.

But Nazis in the supermarket never forget.
Nazis in the supermarket never regret
their past just lapses.

Nazis in the supermarket
skidding on the blood-soaked floor
wade through raw meat.
Nazis crowd in on the clerks, rank on rank,
waving their rain checks,
chanting: The Day of Reckoning is Here.
Our Rage Shall Be Mighty.

Memorize These Simple Signs

...meter and rhyme are seldom used in modern poetry, except in the composition of ballads and light verse... Although no self-respecting poet worthy of his [sic] muse would be caught playing with rhyme today, it remains with us, perhaps as an aural-mimetic phenomenon that could be traced back to the nursery.
— Len Gasparini.

The signs of the road are chiefly these:

The Octagon always means Stop, period.
This is the sign of Completion.

The Inverted Triangle signifies Yield...
This is the sign of Submission...

The Pentagon warns that children may be present.
This is the sign of Subjugation.

The Diamond warns of a Hazard, e.g. Men Working Ahead.
This is the sign of Construction.

When approaching the inevitable curve at the inevitable end of the line

Remember:
1. Don't pass on curves, you can't see what's ahead.
2. Don't cut corners. You can't see what's coming.

Heed the Diamond that warns:
Danger: Rhyme Ahead.
This is the sign of Anticipation.

Such signs tell us
that the future is mapped out,
except that on maps
such lines signify a road to be taken,
a possible course of action to be followed.
The real thing is elsewhere and Other.
The real thing is never actually red,
nor is it half a mile wide or more.
And a town, I should point out,
isn't completely and perfectly round
like it appears on the map.

These are the signs of Convention.

essays in coherence,
all signs in fact read:

This is the sign of Incoherence.

History does not repeat itself.
I repeat:
history does not,
I repeat,
repeat itself.

Check in the mirror
for a sign of Time.
Your mirror will always show you where you've been.

Memorize these simple signs:
Repetition is Addition;
Resemblance is Difference;
Echo is Cause leading to an Inference
that a noise took place.

This is the sign of Retrospection.

It is time
for Rhyme.

This is the sign of Emancipation.

Erect the roadblocks!
Put up the barriers!
Stretch out the nets!
Fasten your seatbelts
and prepare for a   *Collision.*

At the Edge of the World

It was in another landscape
where the mountains had teeth
and the people wore claws and radiation suits.

The sun was setting
there was a chill in the air
and a cold haze fallen over everything.

All the coffee came from vending machines
the gas ran out
the newspapers were yesterday's.

Already the banks had closed for ever
and it was always Sunday.

The credit cards were blocked
our picture IDs were missing
there were storms and betrayals on the horizon.
We were always on alert
but things just kept getting worse.

Still nine hours till dawn
and our eyes would not close down.
There was chatter and static on everybody's brain.

On top of all that
everything we ever wrote
suddenly needed more work.

The stores were shut
the bars deserted.

The roofs were metal
and would boom in the rain
if it ever began.

The ground took a lurch
and sank another foot.

The sea rose again.

There were creatures ready in the woods
just beyond the treeline
a few feet from the houses.

The machinery was all rusted
the car would not start.

Something soft and wet slammed against the windshield
then we dropped the keys
and screamed.

Triptych

I Ecce Ancilla Domini!

It was ten days since the last moon
when, naked under a white robe,
the angel came to her alone like an adulterer,
minutes after her hard-armed husband had left
carrying with him the scent of cedar
and an erection like a piece of dowelling,
puzzling over the mystery
of this strange girl still lying
on white sheets
all these months after the wedding
who would not open her legs to him yet.

The angel dazzled her with a small miracle,
hovered a few inches above the floor,
on faded yellow flames
while her heavy-lidded desire fixed
in startled longing
past the white lilies in the angel's hand.
Then God, a white dove behind her, flew in
over her right shoulder

So much magic is misdirection.

She felt her thighs part.
She was filled and still empty
frozen there transfixed
as if her hands had been nailed to the bed.
She felt history writhe within her

saw the universe change forever.

After the angel left
and she no longer felt the dove
she spread herself
white upon the bed

called silently
for her husband.

Soon, heavy and moon-bellied,
she will whisper to her man
as she measures the heft of him
in her slim hands

and teach him new ways of counting
the days
the years

all the radiant nights to come.

II   Jennifer Catch Had the Look

She had the Pre-Raphaelite look of a water nymph
up to her waist in the pool with her sisters,
pale-skinned, spreading her long red hair
humming through sweet bow lips
to all the silly boys at the edge of the water.

She had the look
of a Rossetti Mary
cowering haloed on the bed
shoulder pressed to the wall
knees parting
eyes fixed well beyond the stem
in the announcing angel's cool hand
wishing to God she was somewhere else
instead of alone in the house
with that terrible man.

She was ethereal;
she hung a towel over the mirror

sometimes lived in the dark,
and one night while I watched
took a shard of glass
and ran it down her arm
deep, just shy of the vein.

Jennifer Catch looked carefully,
found beauty scattering incandescent gleams at her feet,
picked through the shimmering pile of glass
looking for something ragged,
something all edges
and no centre
that spoke
fantastic lambent pleasures to her.

III   Hylas and the Nymphs

It's all Hylas thinks about these days, leaving.

He's tried to tell the man
that he's just not at a stage in his life to settle down yet;
it's not you it's me;
you'll find somebody else who
will give you what you need;
and yes, yes, you're still very attractive.

Hylas turns away tired
from the muscles

and the brawny exploits,
sick of the stench of the Agean stables
that hangs on every inch of the big man's body.

He's tired of the yelling and the fists,
the three-headed dogs,
still has nightmares about those horses
tearing at human flesh
with their yellow slab-like teeth
hooves pulping up the bodies.

The interminable stories he's heard a million times:
— **DID I EVER TELL YOU**
WHAT I DID IN MY
CRADLE?

The air turns thick and green about him
and the girls in the pool
are soft-lipped, small-breasted
pale-skinned and gentle.
Their hands
are slender and clever;
their thighs are deep promises. '

The air hums with lust,
the women's voices are soft,
their faces are smooth, their breath is sweet,

and they speak with their eyes.

Hylas feels his chest give
a lurch,
knowing that the big man
will be beginning to worry now.
But the pool is green and still
he can hardly tell
where the air ends
and the water begins.

City Dining by Jason Tanner

The rage for Northwest cuisine
has settled,
but there's still no substitute
for fresh and local
prepared with imagination, flair.
When you add alder,
the results can be spectacular,
as they are at Orvieto Vissani's newest eatry
Vieni Qui.

I eschew the blue and sweet;
the clarity of a classic martini —
gin, olives, and, I hear, rumours of vermouth —
is a measure of any establishment.

Suffice it to say
Vieni Qui's
is as close to perfection as we can reach
in this fallen world of compromises.

Reluctantly, I restrict myself to a single appetizer
and choose the wild mushroom and red lentil pilaf.
Often, when we're promised wild,
we get the odd cultured oyster or shitaki,
but here are slippery mounds of voluptuous morels,
tender chanterelles
moist with deep history
the taste of ancient woods.

An Oregon Chardonnay proves significant,
golden, fruity, a flirtation with oak in its past.
I am aware of harmonies of melon,
pineapple, gooseberries, unexpected lush asparagus.

My companion, who is late, demands
roasted yam soup,
mineral water,
then falls deathly silent.

The entrée list is impressive
and features many fish;
I settle, however, on the crusted rack of lamb
and a second bottle, an extravagant Zinfandel.

My companion, soup hardly tasted,
finds the choice difficult.
When pressed opts for the blackened halibut
which she dissects
but does not eat,

and informs me
she is involved
with someone else.

The lamb oozes pink.

The server hovers.

The accompanying vegetables
(I pass on the ubiquitous kale) —
rosemary-roasted new potatoes,
carrots in pungent redcurrant glaze —
are excellent.

FUCK DESSERT!

WHAT DO YOU MEAN, "SOMEONE ELSE"?

My companion decides to leave.

The manager quietly accompanies me to the kitchen
where I glimpse a heavenly zabaglione,
a vision coated with finely chopped hazelnuts
and a lubricious ganache.

I see the serving of many meals.

I am told it is late.

A cab is offered at the rear door.

I cannot remember the cost of the fare.

Vieni Qui. Dinner for two, without wine, around $150. Reservations recommended.

Catching Up After Thirty-Three Years

We planned to spend the day catching up
with each other as if
our lives were some sort of obscure race
as if our lives were laundry.

We were two strangers, really,
nothing romantic, never lovers,
we'd be in rooms together,
friends of friends in fact
we barely even spoke back then.

So. Initially, confusion
as we tried to lay out the ground rules,
treading carefully
not knowing what would be turned up
talking around things, about things we could not see, excavating,
unsure of where the point would be,
we circled each other, feinting,
weaving, trying not to land any punches.

We each took care and turns
telling our own stories
each of us stitching together a brief well-edited personal synopsis
all the so-whatever-happened-tos
trying to fix a list of names
sketches of lives lived
a catalogue of marriages, births,
dark tales of scandals, addiction, death, and illness.

A few dead ends
(no pun intended)
loose threads
friends we thought we shared but didn't.
Eventually the first silences
as if there was nothing left to say already.

Once the "catching up" had been done,
respective children counted,

vague faulty memories hunted down
(not many, to be honest),
compared assumptions, shared tastes, now widely diverged,
we found ourselves surprised
at where the time had gone
(hint: nowhere)
so caught up we were in old events.

Parting, we promised
that we would stay in touch,
(as one always does — a lie)
whereas the truth is more
we will never see each other again,
that the day at most has been
an ending, a minor closure
neither of us needed,
a duty done.
But we were strangely grateful
all the same.

And then, goodbye, relief, regret, etcetera.
Walking away, stretching the distance again.
A nagging suspicion
events have overtaken us,
that now this day will call for its own closure,
sometime in the shadowed future.

Our lives fold in and around each others'
because what else do we have?
As soon as we have caught up
we fall behind again
with mighty efforts we halve
the distance and halve
the distance
privately striving, as always,
to understand the why,
to finally get to the point
where the past does not exist
where all history is now.

Injury Time

And now we're into injury time
the last few frantic minutes on failing legs that buckle,
the strain of every breath,
the joints that creak and crack.

He has to see the closing minutes through,
never mind the fucked up knees,
no point in cursing all those sad missed tackles.

It felt like there were clouds for the duration,
leaking a steady drizzle, grey and gloomy,
making the ground heavy
every step a huge, absurd production.

After a strong start,
he began giving away
unnecessary penalties for careless infractions;
unforced errors too numerous to mention,
a heartbreaking own goal,
some pushing, much shoving,

and at least one deliberate foul.

The commentary is timeless;
empty clichés, tired quotations:
"It's not over til it's over, though
looking back, there were a lot of missed opportunities,
and some too-casual play
in the first half.
It's a game of two halves after all
you need to get it in the net
and goals win games
at the end of the day."

At the end of the day
the disappointed crowd stands up and goes,
the light is fading in the west;
the Ref is looking at his watch,

then the final whistle blows.

Passports

They are examining our passports.

They are taking our passports out of the room we are in
to a different room.

We no longer have our passports.

Somebody has taken them away.

Now we will have to wait here until somebody comes for us.

No one will tell us how long we have to wait.

No one will tell us how long we will have to wait.

No one will tell us anything,
and it is dangerous to ask why.

I expect they will come for us soon.

The Woman Who Talks to Her Dog at the Beach

The Woman Who Talks to Her Dog at the Beach
favours the Socratic method:
"Where's your stick?"
"What do you think is going to happen
if you keep chewing on that stick?"
"Would you like a treat?"
"Are you ready to go home now?"

Simple stuff.
(Answers: "The stick is behind me.
Soon it will all be gone.
Yes, always a treat.
No, obviously, home, never.")

But in private, later,
the tricky existential questions fly:
"Who's a Good Dog?"
"Are you a Good Dog?"
"Who's a Good Dog, then?"

The dog wrestles with the questions.

"I have done whatsoever you have asked of me.
I sat when you required it,
stayed, despite my heart being wrenched
with every step you took away from me.
I confess, alone in exile I have often howled
despairing questions of my own:
'Will I never see you again?'
'Are you ever coming home?'
'Why have you forsaken me?'

"I have dropped what you wanted dropped;
searched out and picked up
what was apparently lost —
all the sticks you could not find,

the balls you could not see.
I have rolled over and plunged myself
again and again into the rime-cold ocean
at your behest.

"Yet still you ask the same question:
'Who is a Good Dog?'

"There are other questions.
Clearly, yes, of course
I would like to go for a walk,
and it would be most agreeable
a privilege and an honour
to carry the squeaky toy with me in my mouth.
But am I a Good Dog?
Do you know the answer?
Because I would appreciate some clarity.

"Who, on this shoreline
is a Good Dog?
Are there better dogs than I?
Please, I hope to have an answer
before my coat mats
my legs stiffen,
my breath reeks,
and I am finally ready
to go home at last."

The Woman Who Talks to Her Dog at the Beach
launches her questions into the air.
Life is complicated, and lonely.
There is heartbreak in the future.
People are difficult,
there is great comfort in companionship,
in the simple love of dogs.

Mars Variations

Mars Variations is a time-traveling fractal narrative: a sci-fi horror movie for the ears, referencing works as disparate as Julius Caesar's "Gallic Wars" and H.G. Wells' "The War of the Worlds," Wordsworth's "Prelude," and horror films like Robin Hardy's "The Wicker Man" along with nods towards the various iterations of Godzilla; and of course the classic 1962 "Mars Attacks" Topp's Bubble Gum cards — which form a framing device. The sequence explores the relationship between time, fiction, and facts; between public history and private experience.

As Mars approaches its closest point to the planet Earth, when it is "in opposition," a couple caught in its death rays struggle in a disintegrating relationship; meanwhile, in 1649 an Inspector experiences a different sort of existential struggle as he attempts to complete his report on the senselessly merciless siege of Drogheda in Catholic Ireland by Cromwell and his Protestant army, the Inspector desperately trying to separate facts from vision and myth.

Meanwhile, an alien invasion is underway in a parallel dimension to my own childhood memories of Guy Fawkes celebrations in Scotland — Bonfire Night 1959, commemorating the failed "Gunpowder Plot" of 1605 and the subsequent torture and execution of Guido Fawkes. A straw effigy of Fawkes — a "wicker man" — is burned on a bonfire, a practice which has its origins in prehistory — the ritual bonfires of pagan Samhain celebrations, later appropriated by the 17th-century British government in the service of anti-Catholic propaganda.

Government propaganda is nothing new: the Wicker Man of "history" and the popular imagination is almost certainly a fiction, a product of the attempts of Julius Caesar to defame the Celtic civilizations and the religious beliefs Rome was in the process of conquering and transforming. It is a common theme of early historians to attribute the worst possible barbarism to the conquered: human sacrifice. The Wicker Man straddles time and space in Mars Variations; a monstrous figure, blind, brainless, pure masculinity, pure destruction.

Informing everything is the silence the Japanese have a word for: "ma,"
"significant silence, a pause, the comedian's true skill: timing"; but also
"room," "a space," "opening." The kanji ideogram 間 *can be seen as "sun* 日
in gate" 門.

Thus 間 *is also the blank space on a page of writing, the space between one*
chapter and another, the gap at the end of a line of poetry, for instance, or
the pause the poet takes while reading. A very versatile word, Ma also carries
connotations of the more sinister implications of the distances between
peoples: "hostility," "break," "to sow discord."

As an atemporal fractal narrative, these poems could be read in any order,
shuffled like cards — but the constraints of existence and physical production
mean they have to be presented here as a linear "sequence."

i A Bonfire in the Sky

Turned to blood
the flashlit snapshot gaze of a startled party guest
animal in the headlights before impact
a cyclopean hole drilled through the walls of hell
Mars burns for thirty days and thirty nights
into the bed.

Martian rays scorch the covers
disintegrate flesh
melt muscle and fat from bone.
Witnesses gasp
as skulls are peeled from brains.

At the absolute zero at the absolute centre of our beings
there is the first sense of heat;
we feel the silent ghastly bite
of Martian death rays.

Meanwhile and *meanwhile*
across the centuries merciless
history lurches towards life
drawn to this single point.

ii The End of the World?

On the fifth day the assault will begin.
Hordes stream down to Earth.
Nowhere to hide; no quarter given
in the siege of Planet Earth.

No Surrender!

Politicians swell, blister, blacken, bubble, explode
as ice melts
and the oceans rise like the future.

On the sixth day
bearing down on Tokyo
the tidal wave is coming
big as Godzilla.

Run for your lives, people of Tokyo!
The death of water is a leveller
does what no earthquake could
washing away screaming salarymen
after a timeless instant
in the cool shadow
of the poised wave.

The skyline is sheared

something vaster
more powerful than progress
and far older
stamps on the twentieth century.

iii Attack of the Mole Men
(London: October, 1605)

Underneath the systems
of justice and lawmaking
beneath the seat of oppression

moles at work in stale air.

Secret preparations continue
day and night.

Five men digging
their way into history.
Their heads echo
with the roar of the future
the sound of an explosion
a terrible, limb-tearing
body-splitting
neck-breaking blow
hurling the King into infinity.

Guido Fawkes, the fall guy
measures powder.
Friends look over

hearing the crack of bones
the creak of the thumbscrew
the creak of the rack
the snap of fingers singly breaking
seeing the ribcage exposed
lungs in the air
entrails tossed in the fire.

And Guido, knowing he's being watched
stops what he's doing
smiles his catlike smile
tips his black hat.

iv Evil on the Streets

Edinburgh's dead October streets covered tonight
with curled leaves and the powers of evil.
Malignant dwarves giggling
push old prams.

Inside, the turnip-headed man
lolls like an invalid

not a bone in his body
three hundred years old.

Hey mister
Gie's a penny
fur the Guy.

The streets swarm
with one-eyed pirates
livid grinning clowns
hordes of satanic policemen

streams of executioners
spies cyborgs and psychopathic cowboys.

There are ghosts abroad tonight
there are shadows in the dark on walls
where no light ever falls
obscure as mars black.

Hey mister
Gie's a penny
fur the Guy.

My head is scooped
a single candle
roasts the lid of my blackening skull.

v November Rituals

This is the biggest fire I've ever seen
you need a ladder to get to the top.
We cheered when the Guy arrived
lolling boneless turnip-headed straw man
flayed.

Fireman's carry up the ladder
a rescue in reverse.
The Guy is delivered to flame
eviscerated.

Give me the matches!
The heat!
Keep back sonny
you'll lose your eyebrows!

Rows of bottle rockets
squads of squibs
catherine wheels
sparks fly.

We danced to see the boneshattered villain burn
bound to the stake above us.
We warmed our hands at the past
gorged
smeared with the grease of its glamour
knew nothing

*(they scooped out my head for the candle
flames scorch the lid of my skull)*

On top of the fire
not a bone in his body
the straw man dances down the centuries.

vi Fireside Evenings

We're keeping warm this winter!
Hot and heavy evenings by the fire.
Mulled wine and heated flesh
bodies droop boneless after passion.

Words are spoken.

Come in closer round the fire
watch the dancers in the flames.

Things are seen.

Stare and feel the burnings
feel the heat on your face
see visions past and future.

Life is good tonight.
Roman candles fountain
showers of silver coins.
Sleep is a lifetime away
nothing exists
but this
Now.

High above the city
infinitely happy
we play among the stars.

Reach out a hand
and brush your fingertips
against the dunes and dust of Mars.

vii Scars on the Ground

On the next day, reassessing the hillside
we're surrounded by ghosts.
History takes revenge
history takes no prisoners.
A scorched circle on the hillside shows
perhaps where saucers landed.

Here is the trace of fire
evidence points to the past.
Signs of a disturbance of the earth
an undermining.

Call out the guard and begin to search the cellars.
There is something evil beneath our feet.

viii The Stars Long White Screams of Light

Mars burns red in the sky
a laser sight draws beads
two caste marks of death
two drops of blood
two pinpoints of light between the eyes
of the man and the woman in bed.

In airless space
something bleaker, more pointless than chaos
and more vindictive
takes aim.

This is how evil travels:
projectiles fly to Earth
fast as the speed of light
past Phobos
past Deimos
past Venus
across the solar system in seconds
where the stars are long white screams of light
blast past sleepy lunar colonies
hurtle through the ozone layer
glow red for an instant in the upper atmosphere
punch twin holes in the clouds.

The death touch is coming
the stars have come to Earth, screaming.

Now is the fall of night.

ix Brain Poison

Death beyond sound, death beyond light
faster than thought.
The air parts then claps in the vacuum
in the path of death

and the man and the woman
jerk backwards in bed as if shot.

Spores multiply
tentacles spread poison through the memory banks
coil around the cortex
envelop the cerebellum
choking worms crawling into every fold, crease, and cleft
making all the right connections.
No system on Earth is immune.

Man and woman dream Martian dreams

and rest before the first battle.

x Here Come the Flying Saucers

Indoor fireworks, domestic dispute.
Hate smeared like sweat.
Lungs begin to mutate.

I cannot breathe in this air
there is something wrong with the air
I am smothered in this atmosphere
my eyes sting in this atmosphere.
I cannot close my eyes.

I cannot
cannot
things have not turned out
I do not
I do not understand
I thought
thought I knew what happened yesterday.
This is not what I expected to find
at all.

In anger we say what we mean.
The air is full of china
plates spin like catherine wheels
hurled cups explode like rockets against the wall.

The air is full
of flying saucers.

xi In the Amphitheatre of Infinity
(London: November 7, 1605)

Guy Fawkes is dreaming
a gate
his mother calling.
And in his dream
the gate
                 opens

and Guy looks
                 through

                      the gate
stares
into the sun.

And stares.

. And stares.

                                          間
                                    sun in gate

The second turn to the screws on Guy's thumbs
is a stroke of infinite agony.
He knows now
the universe has become
a steady state of pain
and he is one with the universe.

Nothing has been; nothing will be.
Everything is this
Now.

Pain is Now
the amphitheatre of infinity.

Now comes the third turn.

xii The Old Man Lies about the Past

Come round the fire
and I will tell you about when I was a boy
one night so close to the stars
I touched Mars with my fingertips.

Give me your hands now
we can walk in flames
we can live in fire
and not be harmed.

For we are the dancers in fire
we are those who walk through flames.

xiii A Place of Journeys

Better to live in fire
than die by suffocation.

*(I cannot breathe in this atmosphere
my lungs cannot function in this atmosphere.)*

Look into the flames, love
see the dancers in the fire.
Reach, touch your fingers to the fire that moves;
this is the fire that lives.
You shall not be burned
together we shall not be burned.

Consign yourself to marvellous flame
reach out your hand tonight

and brush your fingertips
across the heat and dust of stars.

xiv The Wicker Man

"...and the pomp/ls for both worlds, the living and the dead."
Wordsworth, The Prelude, 334-5.

In the dying part of the year
on the endless plain
the giant woven man stands massive in my mind.
Ancient, monumental, an anchor.

The Wicker Man stands impassive, hollow
an appetite for sacrifice.

Like the past he has no pity;
he has the stability of myth;
he is what the season demands.
Sanctioned by tradition
we pass through death by fire
into the new year.

xv Like I Was Tokyo, and He Was Godzilla

The Wicker Man
starts to move

crash

PUMPED UP
stamps down
the corridor of centuries.

crash

The Wicker Man
is a big guy.
Lets his fists do his talkin'.
Hey pal
you're history.

PUMPED UP
he's got muscles
an awesome masculinity
is coming like a cliché

crash

to crush the life out of me with his great stupid feet

like I was Tokyo
and he was Godzilla.

CRASH

xvi The Noise Rats Make

Deep in the mind a stirring
scraping sort of movement.
It's the beginnings of a universe
the sound of twigs and dead leaves
the noise rats make.

Treeless hillside   heather   iron skies

over the horizon   across the plain   feet spinning the planet

a giant walking.

The Earth spins like a circus ball
beneath   the feet

that eat

the miles.

xvii The Power of the Past

There's a tearing sound on an empty hillside; under wet
metal sky scrub heather; flat feet twenty miles from toe to
heel suck themselves out of the ground.

As the roots rip you can see that the soles of each foot are a
mass of what looks like white worms: dead white sun-starved
roots squirming like a worried brain in a brainless mass
beneath the feet of the wicker man.

The wicker man begins to move, vast feet propelling the
ground beneath him, spinning the planet beneath his feet
like a circus ball under a clown.

Each step leaves a wet patch of crushed root behind: the feet
trample down the years: the wicker man is the power of the
past: the wicker man is the force of history we summon with
memory.

xviii In the Belly of the Wicker Man

As the wicker man stamps down the corridor of centuries his
belly swells with the past

he feeds on sacrifice and bodies writhe
in the cage of his belly

naked arms mouths thighs breasts buttocks balls stomachs
cocks cunts until the heat becomes unbearable and sparks
begin to fly.

Smoke on the horizon.

The wicker man does not burn.

The wicker man's feet spin the planet and eat up the years
between Then and Now:

the Eternal Present.

He's striding across the land, scooping whole villages up in
fingerless paws cramming whole houses and animals into his
big gob

feasting on women, children dribbling down his chin, old
men's backs snapping like twigs. The fuel of progress.

Nowhere to run; nowhere to hide from the wicker man.

He grinds
he grinds
he grinds
he grinds out lives like cigarette butts.

xix Collection Day

We summon up the past, conjure up ghosts, write the wicker man
into the years, engrave the nightmare on our consciousness.

Time is delivered, carried in the wicker man's belly/we put out
the path for the wicker man's feet to find/this is what we call
logic/sense/pattern on chaos/meaning/heritage/civilization/
this is how we write the universe/create the spinning ball of
molten rock that fires off planets.

The wicker man touches the stars.

The wicker man is coming and our creation will kill us/the past
is on a collision course with a single instant/power/strength/will:
all pin-headed stupid blind instinct; all single-visioned cyclopean
vast masculine power on a collision course with Now.

You have remade the universe and it's coming to get you.

Collection Day is here.

xx Nothing More than Memory

as he turns away in silence there is an instant in the cool watery afternoon sunlight that shines through the half-opened door, slides across the living room floor and slithers up the side of the refrigerator when she thinks she sees a wisp of straw escaping from his collar. She shivers with fear because she knows now he will eat her alive.

Touching the giant blank dry face shows you it's nothing: an old haystack maybe; a pile of dry twigs. One touch and he flies into a million million pieces back to chaos, folds up without a whimper.

Nothing. Just sticks on an open field. Good kindling.

Nothing more than memory; just a loose weave; superstition; propaganda.

xxi Cromwell's Prayer
(Drogheda, Ireland: September, 1649)

It was in the final days
that last endless night
in our camp near the walled city
when I was deep in prayer.
An hour before dawn
a mighty wind arose from the centre of darkness.

The guy ropes groaned, and the tent was a lung
filled with the breath of God. And my spirit
was opened unto the firmament of heav'n,
unto the fiery sun and ice cold moon
even unto the stars spangling the hemisphere,
the holy campfires of God's great army.

Shouts of heavenly warriors filled my ears
as the tent was filled with the breath of God
as my mind was filled with the wisdom of God
as my spirit was filled with the words of God
as the sky swelled with the screams of sinners
a blessed hymn of praise.

I gave thanks unto my Lord
for I am His mighty sword forged in his similitude.
I looked on the city of Drogheda

and stretched out my fist to smite it.

I am the citycrusher
I breathe cleansing fire
on my lips death's kiss
my mouth approaches, whispers
I am Juggernaut, eldest of things,
my wheels will grind your bones to paste.

xxii Spoils of War
(Drogheda, Ireland: September 11, 1649)

You get what you can in these situations.

The siege was almost over
and the city was not a rich one
so when we heard about the gold
yes we said yes.

They said it is hidden.
We said we shall find it.
They said well hidden.
We said tell us
(then we broke a finger or two).
They said the one-legged man.
We said we see him.
They said the wooden one is hollow.
We said we know what to do.

He screamed.
I pinned him with my pike.
He wriggled.
The others tore off the peg leg.

Rage, rage.
It was as solid as a tree.

So I took the wooden leg, laughing
bastard we'll teach you Irish bastard
clubbed him with the thing
spilled his brains out on the rock
smacked his skull open like a nut
cracked him like an egg
went about God's business
lingered to watch the fire around the tower
where we were burning the rest of those barbarous wretches.

The General said
it was God's righteous judgement
on the miserable sinners.
And God had told him so.
We had his word on that.

xxiii Angels of the Air
(Drogheda, Ireland: September 11, 1649)

Then I was taken unawares
thinking, strangely, of my dead wife
as she was in the dear early days
when she had a great beauty.
I was drawn apart from battle
to a pleasant light-filled room. Many people.
Among them all we danced as if alone.
We glowed. Her secret taste was on my lips
lips parted, tongue touched teeth, flicked ... found entry
hands covered breasts
cleaving to me
she thrust, she thrust.

Like witches we rose together and danced in the firmament
magnificent star-folk we, brilliant angels
sphere-dwellers.
Ah, the air! Those angels of the air!

Time passed.

Out of silence a monster grunted on my left
drumbeat of chaos, destiny lurched towards me
a stupid drunken one-eyed giant
a hammer in his vicious fist.

I heard the great belch of a cannon

and watched a lump of iron swell
first a mote three hundred feet away
then an iron eye opening
finally a lazy balloon puffed up with death
that floated through space
falling, hardly turning
o, it is coming, it is coming, I sang to myself
as the ground swelled and met my feet
directly in its path.

In an instant
where once my mother's hands caressed,
tweaked and chased my toes
called them pigs,
flesh and blood were gone
chewed, pulped to bloody meat
smashed, splintered
my feet and ankles ground to nothing.

I felt no pain.
I knew my God had chosen me for this,
this plotted intersection, from my birth.

Above my stumps of shattered bone and sinew
tendons flapped like rags against my bloodied calves
my body swayed
and I began to dance in a burning ocean of my own life's blood.
I dealt death to Cromwell's men
I danced, I danced a warrior's dance.

Cut to head. I parry.
My riposte (cutover, lunge, one-two) parried;
back en garde, parry, redouble
(beat attack, feint to head, draw parry,
cut to arm, sever hand at wrist);
parry, disengage, step back
slip under clumsy beat attack
flèche (point attack), pierce chest, lungs.
Hiss of escaping air.
I deal death. I cannot die.

Sword in my hand
sick with delight
I dance out eternity
on jagged pegs of bones and blood.

xxiv In a Place of Many Paths
(The Inspector's First Report)

Yes, Masters, a straightforward assignment,
I told them. But you cannot trust a path.
Reach the city, record the facts, return.
I was too confident, that much I'd admit;
but the weather turned quickly vile,
and something happened to our road.

For a few miles at first our way looked clear,
even through the solid slapping sheets of rain
that set our tired horses shivering,
driving waves that wrapped themselves around our bodies,
until it seemed we stalked the ocean's floor.

Suddenly the wind died.

The rain poised in the air hung drop on drop,
we in its shadows and everything naked,
singular. I saw into the heart of things,
even into my own unworthy heart
where no blood moved.

Then rain again, again wind
and, horribly, a landscape choked with paths,

tendrils writhing across the countryside,
and no way clear.
Behind us, vinous, more roads mocked us,
fingers splayed, grasping, throttling.
I knew at once
that we were lost forever in a place of many paths.

xxv Paths Meet in the Place of Death
(The Inspector's Second Report)

We made our way there
by every possible path,
but the place was always the same
where we paused in the silence and the smell of smoke;
a point everywhere, nowhere, minutely advancing.
Silence drifted between particles.

At the convergence of vortices,
I saw my back retreating
into the future
explode like a rocket
into a million million sets
of possible shoulders, sets
of swinging purposeful arms,
as many as the stars.

Behind me a million million men
approaching by many paths
wound together
until the path was my path,
and the moment was Now.

I am the waist of an hourglass,
the steady point where the future becomes
the past. Where each grain

    drifts

        past

           me

              past

           me

       pours

    the future.

xxvi Sum Over Histories
(The Inspector's Third Report)

Nothing had happened
until I made it happen.
Bones and bodies; chaos, fragments, sticks and whispers.
Events waiting to have existed.
Nothing would happen
before I made a move,
picked my way between possible paths,
opened my mouth, entered speech,
moved my feet through piles of words,
sent sound scattering
towards the future.

I will set it all down here:
the true story of a one-legged man
and a man with no feet;
the innocent burning;

the burning tower;
thousands dead.
Suppression, extinction, horror, apocalypse.

And that man Cromwell best knows his own thoughts;
which were his and which were God's.

I do not trust the evidence of my own ears;
I do not trust my eyes' evidence
but I will set it down here;
I will set it all down here.

Weak afternoon sunlight
shining through
shattered city gate.

Death
in mouth.

xxvii **Death's Pendulum**
(The Inspector's Last Report)

Masters:
my journey was indeed a strange one,
beyond me.

I could write of where or when

of the fractured beauty at the ragged margins of my existence;

of the space between one second and the next when the ratchet
paused poised on the cog of the clock's wheel shudders, tips
over, and the hand moves

once

again

of the moment when the pendulum finds peace, hangs in the
air without weight

again —

(this is where I locate time
in space
Now
before the assertions of force)

but this is not in my brief,
Masters.

A strange journey indeed. Everything in doubt.

Each time we measured the road even
it seemed a little longer, and a little longer,
and we are drawing ever

far
a

                                                        part.

I could write of reasons,
but I saw only results,
and those but dimly
as it were through smoke,
and, as I write, as always,
the odour of roasted flesh within me.

I fear I am lost, Masters,
and will linger here forever
a wretched animal in these ruins
this rubble my memory.

I am become death
not able to travel far from this place,
from these scattered city walls,
from this infinite border,
before I am doomed to return;
the hills around are grown too sheer.

Let us then consider chaos;
let us dwell on strange attractions,
Masters.

I could write of when
but the time is
always
never
Now.

This is my doom,
my wyrd.
I am a hanged man swaying
restless
Death's Pendulum.

xxviii Pod Creatures Ate My Baby
(Next Year)

Then, dawn, thereabouts, trucks brought in wrecking crews
for the big demolition job. Long overdue
jackhammers, cats, and backhoes
started ripping down the walls and doors.

Now, all over the city, like dots on the tube,
like fillers on the evening news,
apartment blocks in vague explosions
collapse in puffs of rising dust.

Big drills smash through sidewalks
angry wasps banging their business ends down,
mechanically pounding the golden streets
that shatter like sheets of cheap toffee.

The drills grind on into the motherlode
into the telephone lines
into the veins of rich copper, into the bubbling babble
the burbling babel of chattering urban blood.
In the end the circle turns on itself
the city eats itself at last.

As night stumbles, droops, and falls
jerking in cardiac arrest,
mutant Martians in search of fine dining crawl out the cracks.
Cyborg werewolves sharpen titanium claws

and multi-eyed baby-eating pod creatures
stomp down ruined streets, scaly, horny,
looking for longlegged rabid ratsucking hookers from Venus
just in off the evening shuttle
shivering, strung out on drugs from another galaxy
going cryogenic turkey
in the meantime snorting freezedried Big Macs
—the good stuff you can't get on Venus.

Stand back when that special sauce hits those Venusian mucus
membranes pal!
If you value your sanity.

Some of us got the hell out just in time,
holed up with the kids in the hills.
Bruised and abraded psyches aching,
watching the fading city burn,
we dreamt of what seemed real.

In the stove, fire; in the fire, flames;
in the window, fire's reflection
flickering round your head, flickering round the baby's head.
Thus the moment's satisfaction
watching the flames of our reflected fire
appear suspended like desert miracles in the trees,
and the trees stand still.

Thus, slowly, it comes to me,
slowly, as I watch, it comes to me,
that this is the good and the word of god to me;
this is as good as god.

xxix The End

time to close the case
packing for a return journey
to a place that no longer exists

what might have been magic
is after all a sphere lined with mirrors
where all light is turned back on itself
in the absolute dark of the centre
a point of impossible power focussed
beyond
me

meanwhile and *meanwhile* and *meanwhile* and *meanwhile*
aliens trudge up ramps to spacecraft, sullen,
defeated by some intractable earthly phenomenon
or other.

meanwhile and *meanwhile* and *meanwhile* and *meanwhile*

fires die
rockets sputter

drop to earth

the final piece of human offal is thrown in the final fire
crowds dissolve, return to life
lose interest in the limbless lump of body at their feet,
beneath the scaffold, beneath the sky
in front of the cathedral
at the centre of the city
one fine November morning

gates open
governments resume
order is restored
antidotes discovered

if this is not the end of the world
what is?